Pieces to Peace

Copyright © 2019 by Anthony Donaghue

All rights reserved.

This book or any portion thereof
may not be reproduced or used in any manner
whatsoever
without the express written permission of the
publisher, except for the use of brief quotations
in a book review.

Printed in the United States of America

First Printing, 2019

ISBN 978-0-359-34740-7

http://www.lulu.com/spotlight/artbyant

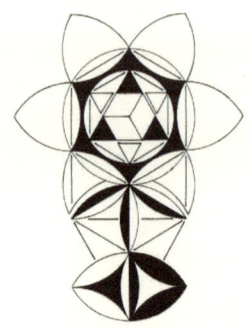

"Dear Mother…"

Dear Mother, you taught me to watch over my sister and brother,

Dear Father, you taught me to stand strong and not to bother,

Dear God, you taught me how to be and how to see,

You gave me tools to set myself free,

All these rules trick the fools before they see potential,

The trickery is mental,

I get paid for my time like a rental,

Standing in the truth, it's central,

I watch for honesty and speak honestly,

Sometimes the truth hurts,

You were meant to see,

Not to follow blindly, I aim to put it kindly,

Sometimes the message is misunderstood,

Never mind me,

It's all smoke and mirrors,

Until your focus clears,

The truth appears,

All the fear and sadness disappears,

Passion steers and turns the gears,

Love will fill your ears,

Joy will fill your tears,

A new beginning nears after all these years of work and devotion,

Pouring glasses of emotion,

Taking on the vastness of the ocean,

Before learning how to swim,

Going out on a whim to put plans in motion,

Silently starting commotion amidst the masses wasting away as time passes,

More things, more strings,

We're all tied up,

Carrying an empty cup,

Full of thoughts and things,

Neither listen as our heart sings,

My ears ring as I focus on the frequency that's frequently seeking me,

The angels reaching out,

Speaking about all the love and light that keep us shining bright for others to muster might amidst their flight through the dark night of the soul,

As they rise from the hole of society,

To the whole of piety,

I'll never go quietly,

There's a fire blazing inside of me,

I never knew the power of poetry,

The weight of the words was crushing me,

Left unwritten or unsaid,

I'd surely be dead,

As the mind is fed,

Thoughts become lead,

Creating a heavy head,

A tragic bed,

Which can be fled with mighty magic,

Led by a light heart,

I'm a lover so I tend to fight smart,
Even embers could make a blaze start,
Odd how my mind remembers ways of art,
Years apart from the maze start,
I'm picking fears apart,
Watching as my love steers the dart,
Clearing the doubt that I couldn't figure out,
As the energy around me clears,
Sounds of love and joy surround me,
Focused on my will to fulfill my dreams,
Even, against all odds,
It seems I always find the silver seams,
Following the flow of conscious streams,
I'm in it to win it,
No matter how you spin it,
The vortex in my cortex striving toward the apex of what my cause affects,
my mind selects and the heart directs, before the balance,
It was quite a complex that used to perplex my being,

As I reach for the sky,
I'm clearly seeing that I was never shy,
Rather, I was coerced into a shell,
In a well-versed attempt to keep me in hell,
I used to cry and wonder why you left,
The light never did,
Born to fly,
The light never hid,
Even as I placed my heart in the chest,
Locked the lid,
True beauty resides inside,
Passion decides and purpose confides,
This painful path is straight and narrow,
Directed to the heart like a flaming arrow,
I'm never switching sides,
Always making strides,
Regardless of the changing tides,
I know where deception hides,
My eternal gratitude to the angelic guides watching over me on these wild rides.

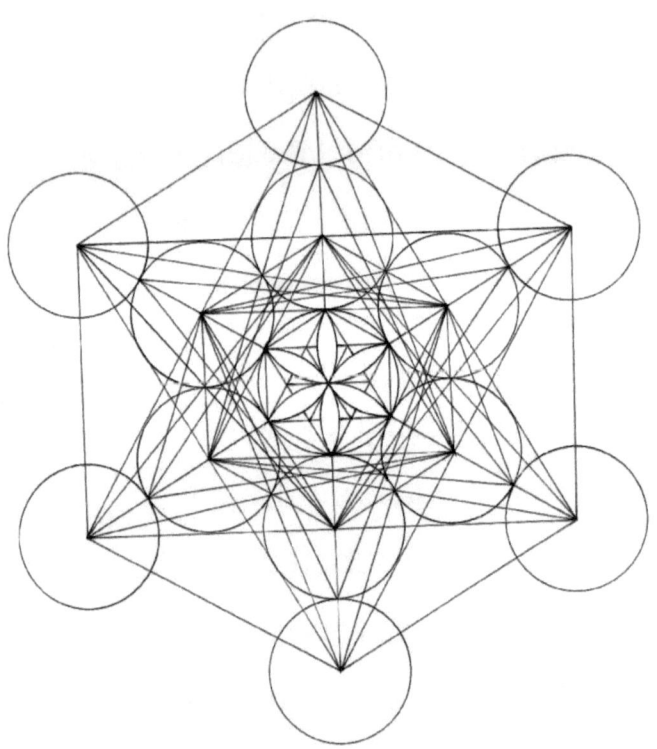

"Testing…"

The lowest I've felt in a while,
The lord led me through,
Allowing me to see what's true,
Forgiveness for forgetfulness,
Freedom from fears,
Comforted by compassionate ears,
You can't trust your thoughts,
Deception lies in sneaky spots,
As we live and learn,
We connect the dots,
As we give, we earn,
We return to our youth,
The truth,
In the eyes of a child,
Life is filled with love and light,
Clear skies on a dark night,
Full moon, stars in sight,

No worries of wrong, or right,

Just a curious mind,

Shining bright for those of us on our way home,

We walk this line of time to help those in need as we let go of greed,

When we let her lead,

God has a plan for us all,

After all, this life is a testimony to her glory,

The places I've been, the situations I'm in,

Undoubtedly planned by a goddess,

Leading me through loving lessons,

Guiding me to give to those in places different than my own,

Messages in a comforting tone,

A billion of us with beauty in every bone

We overcome all that stands in our way,

Progress through process,

Abundance and prosperity through clarity,

If doubt comes twice,

We count our blessings thrice.

"Fire and Freedom"

Pen to the page, these thoughts never age,
They inspire rage,
If I don't free them from the cage,
An actor,
Actively seeking freedom from the stage,
The wandering worries of a worker's wages,
A student of the mystics and mages,
Wisdom and wonder fill my cup,
As I turn the pages,
I'm looking up and feeling down,
Looking down and feeling up,
Thinking back but moving forward,
If they were right,
How come I left?
Maybe all that's left, is right,
Maybe I'm addicted to the night,
Also, to the light,

Maybe I love how they "fight",
Patience, the story is unraveling,
Lessons learned from traveling,
Have faith, it's all worth the wait,
Trusting the timing lessens the weight,
An eye for an eye,
The whole world blind,
A lie for a lie makes the truth real shy,
My heart and hope have risen,
From the ashes of a fierce fire,
I shine my light into the prism,
Escape the prison,
Transformation of desire,
As the smoke clears,
I admire a view of beauty and elevation,
Ignoring retaliation,
Remain peaceful and patient,
The gains were massive,
The attacks were passive,
Slaves to the wages,

Hearts fill the shelves,

As we fear to be courageous,

Outrageous,

I hope the disease isn't contagious,

I'm detached,

Made it through a war, unscratched,

Unmatched by the demons,

Scheming on my downfall,

Screaming as I'm still standing tall,

My life changed with one call,

As the shadows started to fall,

I put my life on the line, learning lessons about these blessings of mine,

Allowing the light to shine,

Reflecting in the night time,

Waiting for the right sign,

It's fine,

I know right where I left mine.

"7 years"

We're here to learn the effects of mindless aggressions through mindful confessions,

A trial by fire burns away our obsessions with physical possessions,

What's mine is yours,

What's yours is mine,

There comes a time,

When all is stripped away,

The lines are blurred,

Black and white turn to grey,

Night or day, the light leads the way,

When things get dark,

We learn to pray,

When I lay to rest,

I'm at peace knowing I did my best,

Honesty, integrity and intention,

Keys to the test,

Honor and trust will bring joy home to nest,

All this time I was living dead,
Couldn't escape my head,
My family and friends break the bread,
I make gold from lead,
Never felt safe but the safe is in my head,
The vault of heaven opens at eleven eleven,
The gears begin turning,
The fears are burning,
Silence speaks secrets,
The seekers of seven,
Creation and consumption,
Continually balanced,
Maintaining the state of mind,
to mind the state of creation & destruction,
A perpetual cycle,
Unlearned lessons recycle,
Transform the spiteful energy,
Allow their deception,
No place in your perception,
A pause to praise,

A peaceful tone in reception,

It heals my heart of stone,

Lost in focus,

The silence starts to drone,

Elevation of vibration, changes in sensation,

Fluid situations of celebration,

In an ocean of motion,

Joy ignites commotion among those who cannot control emotion,

Frequencies frequently varying from foods and fasting,

Ingesting information,

Inspiring a life everlasting,

A journey from knowledge to wisdom,

Understanding,

Relationships are demanding,

We're open with our feelings,

To help others healing.

"The wise rise..."

Open and willing to speak about the topics
that are chilling to most,

Rise and greet us with love,

They wanted to speak up,

When push came to shove,

The noise would rise above their voice,

A feeling of doubt in the choice,

Until we rejoice in the awareness,

Presence of presents in the present,

The eternal moment gives us limitless power
to awaken those who feel misunderstood,

Each carrying a piece to the puzzle
that's puzzling our peace,

Enough muzzling the beast,

We've taken part from a liar's heart,

Never fear a fresh start,

"These are my people and this is my art",

Standing here and branding fear,

This is my life, I choose to steer,
Listen closely,
Angels whisper in your ear,
There's a message that only you can hear,
A vision for you,
The passionate seer,
Speaking words of wisdom in rhyme,
They surely appear in time,
Your love is light,
Shine bright my dear,
The wise rise from the dead,
The fool cries from the bed he made,
Paralyzed by fear and lies of the head,
The truth can be read,
but never said,
For those of Babylon will babble on,
They're never bored of the game aboard,
As you walk the plank,
Thank the lord,
She freed you of their cursed sWord,

Even against a hoard of men,
My angels cut the cords again,
I'm a weird one and the odd man is out,
But, without the doubt,
I never would have gone in,
Living it up, they're dying down,
Walking on water, pretending to drown,
Give it a rest,
We're eternally blessed,
This is all a test,
Take the weight off your chest,
Nouns will never affect your crown,
You're moving too fast to focus,
Just slow down.

"Head:Game…"

Drugs taught me about escaping reality,
Harry Houdini, until I met the genie,
"One wish, what will it be?"
Suddenly, it all made sense to me,
What we often fail to see,
The things we love,
Are the things that come to be,
We forget what it's like to be free,
Running away in a search for relativity,
Clarity resides in creativity,
A natural mechanism for coping,
The tool of all transformation,
We're meant for constant elevation,
Salvation through celebration of information,
Acquiring knowledge and wisdom leads to elation,
Generation of opportunity through relation,

As we learn and teach,

We expand our reach while growing the community,

There's limitless power within love and unity,

We each have a life to lead beautifully,

Showing others to accept their sisters, brothers, fathers and mothers,

True love is unconditional,

Moderation is key to experiencing bliss,

Exhaustion causes remorse,

Laziness sparks envy,

Enjoy the moments,

Without pretending that all good things… are ending,

The cycles never stop,

The light is always bending,

New scenes for spiritual mending,

Abundance is your prop,

Plant your seeds and harvest your crops,

As the leaves change,

Temperature drops,

Life teaches that the beauty grows,

As light goes through darkness,

Nature sings and silence rings,

As soul springs back to things,

The cold and dark come for reasons that we come to know,

A time to change and grow,

Embracing the storm,

Even if it feels strange,

A need to rearrange our focus,

See beyond the hocus pocus,

The state of lack causes a crack in faith,

Feeling late but we won't attack,

We must sit back and attract.

"heArt…"

Words unsaid hurt the most,

As we hold in emotions,

Hearts start to roast,

A toast of lovers but the truth uncovers,

Her boast to others,

A lesson in love,

A message from above,

Her focus was below the covers,

All curtains raised, respects were paid,

The peace was praised,

It remained unfazed,

Our feelings must be honored,

Lest we are stealing the joys we pondered,

On the streets I have wandered,

I wondered what life had in store for me,

Whether I should tether my wealth to a reflection of myself,

Motions made in stealth propelled my mental health,

The truth set me free,

The key to safety,

Hidden safely in creativity,

The vault of heaven,

Hidden in sight,

For those seeking insight,

Door eleven, floor seven,

Learn to balance four and seven,

There comes a time to love and let go,

People, places and things,

Help us move and grow,

If we surrender to the waters of life,

We will surely flow,

Right where the lord needs us to go,

Assistance becomes style,

Resistance becomes futile,

Years of denial,

I sat through my trial,

God as my judge,

The devil advocated all the roles,

I won't entertain endless rabbit holes,

Honesty and integrity through the polls,

The world told me what to be,

Silence freed me,

Praise the lord,

Raised the sword and cut the cord,

Allowing me to walk through the flames,

A blaze burning away all that I AM not,

Leaving me with the truth of all that I AM,

I AM all of that,

Confident in creating a life of abundance,

In correspondence to the creator that created me,

A healer, a feeler and a lover,

Set us free,

Lessons learned,

Listening when God called me.

"Never fear a fresh start..."

God shows me the beauty of the world,
Inside and out,
I've seen life from a less traveled route,
Overcoming fear and doubt,
The challenges come and go,
However, the blessings stay forever,
Wisdom and comprehension,
Quiet the apprehension,
Acquiring knowledge,
Consciously & constantly,
Changing everything I thought life to be,
Fallacies of freedom,
Following false flags,
Price tags & body bags,
Nature is calling,
We're busy stalling,
Blind to the fact,

Ignoring God's call,
The one where she promises it all and more,
We can't buy that in a store,
Stay humble,
Feet on the floor,
You'll see blessings galore,
Life is playing out in beautiful ways,
Waiting on you to admire and adore it,
We were taught to ignore it,
Always searching for the next door,
Life is a play with actors and scenes,
Playing roles and chasing goals,
The tables turn as the bridges burn,
That's how the scene goes…
Applause from the back rows,
Silence from the front rows,
Everyone in front knows,
Right where the knife goes,
Even friends can be foes,
Stay on your toes,

They say we're friends,

Sometimes, I pretend,

I cannot lend my energy to bend into something I'm not over what they thought,

I triple what I brought so I'm giving a lot,

Don't take it lightly, I won't lose my spot,

I won't go politely cause they're slow to invite me but quick to spite me,

Not sure how to feel,

I thought the pain was real,

I pick and peel what I used to conceal,

The layers unfold speaking of lairs untold,

Mighty and bold, I broke the mold,

Aware of the power I hold,

Losing my grip yet gaining control,

Service and soul from the black hole,

In which we were whole,

Tricked to pay a toll,

We're the fools who play for gold,

We don't do as we're told.

"E(nergy)motion"

Time and energy are one and the same,

We use them both,

Maneuver through levels of the game,

Explore and expand your horizons,

Courage is commended,

The road less traveled,

Once unraveled,

Leads back to the source,

Many lessons in force,

As we complete the course,

Curiosity was killing us,

The inspiration is filling us,

Spilling out from these thrilling adventures,

Our freedom frees them,

The knowledge will feed them,

The stories we wrote,

The wisdom we tote,

On a journey with no destination,

Each location inspires desires for information,

In a nation of stagnation,

I'm channeling change,

As a I move through the matrix,

Pay close attention,

Every liar has their ticks,

Like every magician has their tricks,

As life moves on,

The mind, body and heart work as one,

If one is off slightly,

We feel tied up tightly,

Intense energies and friendly enemies,

We must love them all,

Unless we want to fall,

Confidence and trust keep us walking tall,

Without faith, we're left with worry,

Mind in a flurry to keep our vision blurry,

We were taught to live in a hurry,

Everything wants us to speed up,

God wants us to slow down,

Allowing guidance to flow,

Through our crown,

Choosing a smile instead of a frown,

Believe you will walk on water,

You will not drown,

Keep looking up without backing down,

If we don't know what's best,

We repeat the test until we learn the rest,

We are our own best friend,

Our worst enemy,

The struggle between light and dark will never end.

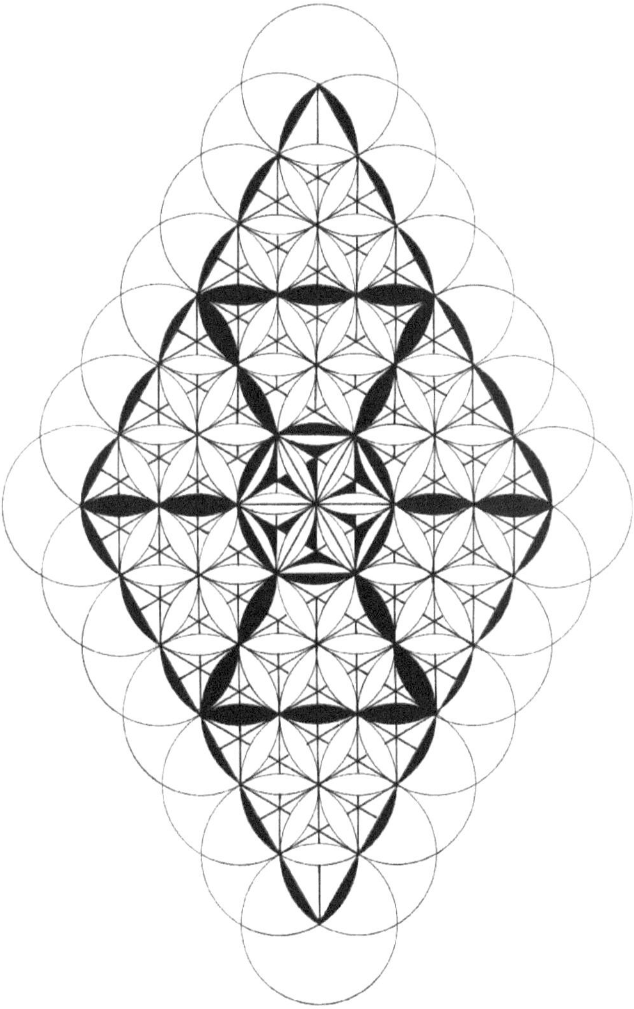

"Reali(TV)"

It's hard to watch the characters get tired,

I admire my life to stay inspired,

My heart takes the lead,

Reading signs my mind can't conceive,

The magic I breathe helps me believe,

Miracles I receive,

Relaxing and attracting,

Relief for the restlessness,

Impacting my life through crafting,

Drafting plans to stop attempts at turning life into a repeating cycle of competing psychos,

In the moment,

I see all the love,

Blessings from above,

Oppressing the stressing thoughts,

As I connect the dots,

I'm untying the knots that had me tied up,

I freed my hands,

No demands if you don't support the plans,

Fans fill the stands,

Strands of source,

Exerting force to follow course,

The chain that binds us loosens,

As we look to the light that blinds us,

We must seek wisdom to be wise,

Focused and fearless,

We sift through the lies,

We lift our eyes from the ties below,

to the heavens above,

Lessons of love never lessen the love,

In the moments of doubt,

Watch how things play out,

Don't say a word,

Maybe you can't trust what you heard,

It's absurd to follow the herd,

I've seen the ways of the wicked,

Waging wars on the warriors of peace,

All for a piece of pernicious pie,
But I… must trust that all is just,
An eye for an eye leaves us shy of the vision,
Only causing more division,
The faithful fly,
I believe in my decision,
The past has passed,
No need for revision,
After the last incision,
I'm cutting ties with precision,
This is my remission,
Tricks of the trade,
Make the master a magician,
They said life isn't fair,
Who are we to compare?
Moving here and there,
Through the circus to find out how to be,
Clowns control what you see,
Steady your stare with a breath of fresh air,

Dare to bare your weakness,
Strength through meekness,
Share your uniqueness,
A gift to lift others above their doubts,
Fear comes for all,
Tears start to fall but we don't stop brawl,
Focused on the silent call that reminds us there is no wall,
These blessings been a long time coming,
I spent a long time running,
Waiting patiently, in a long line,
Gunning for the top,
I'll never stop,
If I play my cards right, I'll win it all tonight,
Left it all up to fate,
God fills my plate,
Never a second too late,
My faith is great,
I made it through the wait,
Now that I'm weightless,

They extend the hate,

I won't take the bait,

I already ate, there's no debate,

I was taught to work hard for what I wanted,

Taunted by thoughts of not enjoying the life I'm living, giving my all to answer the call,

Get the ball rolling,

I'm bowling for answers,

The pins are like dancers,

I need to strike out,

Digging deep I struck doubt,

Hoping that I luck out,

Maybe my peers were right,

A fool who brought a light to a gun fight,

In hindsight a weapon is worthless if you're blind, right?

The truth is,

The youth is…

A weapon of mass construction,

Victims of violence,

Raised to praise destruction,
Induction to a society that ignores piety,
They lied to me,
Would have died to make cents,
Then I made sense of what was inside of me,
I'm in love with my life,
I keep a knife close to cut cords of strife,
I won't entertain stress in my life,
A rite of the righteous,
To accept my rights,
I write my wrongs into songs,
Shine light into the nights of depression,
Express your aggression,
Your heart knows where it belongs,
All that suppression,
Oppression of the soul,
We're bound to pay the toll,
We came to lose our mind,
Don't dig the hole deeper,
Find your love and awaken the sleeper,

I made friends with the reaper,

He said,

"they're all dead, living lies is costly,"

For a second, he lost me,

"but what did the truth cost me?"

He replied, "nothing, but many have died in pride searching for passion and purpose"

"in the Darkness"

This time,
"right now,"
It always is,
A place to vow passion and devotion,
Immersed in consciousness,
An intense responsiveness,
All the things that are,
All the things that were,
Whirring by as I focus on the place,
Stirring up commotion as I race,
One second I'm there,
The next, I'm gone,
This journey I'm on,
Never leads me wrong,
It amuses the muse inside of me,
Creating song of the vision I see,

Without division,

Quickly,

Shifting my perspective,

Leading myself to the objective,

I stay protected,

A light reflected from a knight selected,

Bright and white, a light connected,

All that's without, is within,

All that is end, begins,

These wins ride the winds,

Feeling the skin of a goddess,

Feeling modest, but let's be honest,

I'm in your head, silent, but your eyes said,

I'm a book that you haven't read,

All these words and pages,

What if I don't want to share?

Let's not compare, let's create,

Let's celebrate, a date to remember,

Remembering the dates,

When we lost track of time and dates,

As my mind skates down the road,
The images load,
Welcome to my humble abode,
These pieces of peace come to be,
Sometimes contradictory,
I lost the race and found victory,
Oh, what a mystery,
A miss to be,
A mist of me,
I wish to be pure divinity,
Expressions of infinity,
The eternal energy,
Exposing the external enemy,
Words wave through the waters,
A message of the forgotten daughters,
A goddess,
Praise her ways,
She made it,
Through days of darkness,
A haze of starkness,

Light the way, fight to stay,
Sometimes there isn't words to say,
Let the scene play on,
Move along, keeping strong,
It's never too late to change your fate,
Longing for lights, love and liberty,
Long nights, above a beautiful ink,
The sights of joy,
Create and Destroy,
Masterpieces of magic,
Pieces of a magic master,
Placed on paper through pen,
Remember the time when,
I don't remember time then,
Nonexistent measure,
The number one stressor, a compressor,
Little bottles on a dresser,
Maybe they'll ease the pressure,
I'm focused on the treasure,
It's been a pleasure.

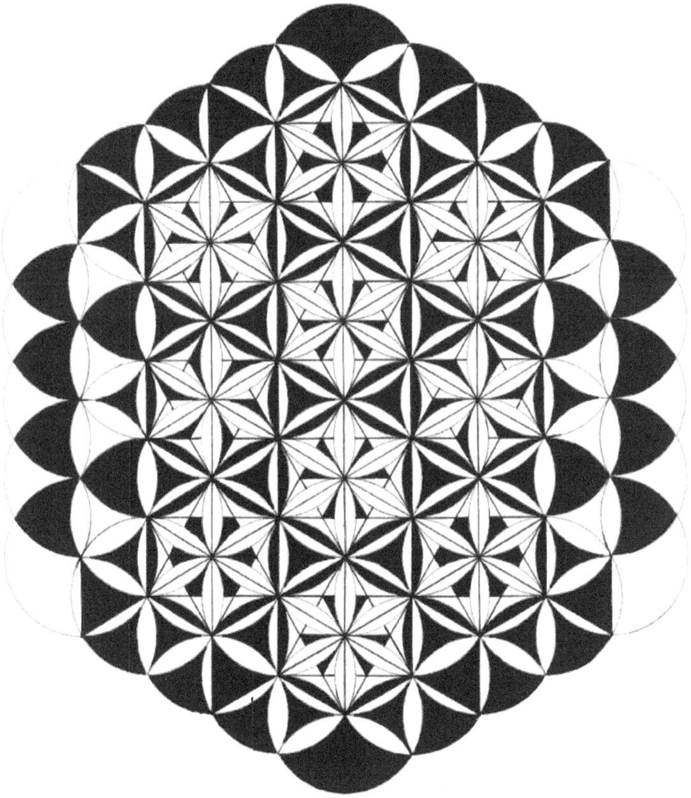

"Vision"

It's a game,

We're the same,

But different,

I aim, to see potential,

Moving through the gears,

Sequential,

Motions become essential for the mental,

Basically fundamental,

Fun – da – mental,

The mind, how fun,

Personality? Which one?

Shifting through the tune in my ears,

Lost too soon, lifting through tears,

After years, the fears tremble,

Eyes resemble the sun,

They're set ablaze from the gaze of one,

An ant set out to move a ton,

Lost in the fun of the run,
Head low, eyes in the sky,
Eagle's view, details renew,
Review the motive,
Secrets explosive,
Casually confidential,
Powerful potential,
sWords of silence,
The world of violence,
A dedicated science,
Prone to defiance,
It relies on compliance,
Alliance according to reliance,
Independent yet dependent,
Heaven sent on being hell bent,
Keen to the scent of trouble,
The opportunities double,
We're meant for more,
But less opens the door,
What's in store is stored in,

A place where the four is foreign,
Stability relies on the ability,
To maneuver with agility,
Pressures process as plays for progress,
Out of the woods and in to the fire,
There's no cure for desire,
Pure intention to acquire love,
Attention above all,
Watching the fall slowly,
The terrain is holy,
The quiet rain will hold me,
Someone told me the key to voodoo,
"Time stops when you do,
As the light moves through you,
Insight comes to you",
Standing still, I move the most,
Outstanding will to stand the roast,
Pain and Prosperity both at hand,
Choices demand commitment,
Commanding curiosity,

Persistent,
Resistant to assistance,
Assistant to resistance,
This vision is valuable,
Priceless and malleable,
A reaction to attracting,
An attraction to reacting,
A fraction of distraction,
Loss of traction,
Inspired action turns the wheels,
Energy in motion,
Electric feels,
As the body heals,
The mind reels the film of life,
Blind to the kind of beauty behind us,
There's a need for your seed,
Plan to plant love for those in need,
The power of greed cannot take the lead,
As we wander through waves of light,
The sun comes to save the night.

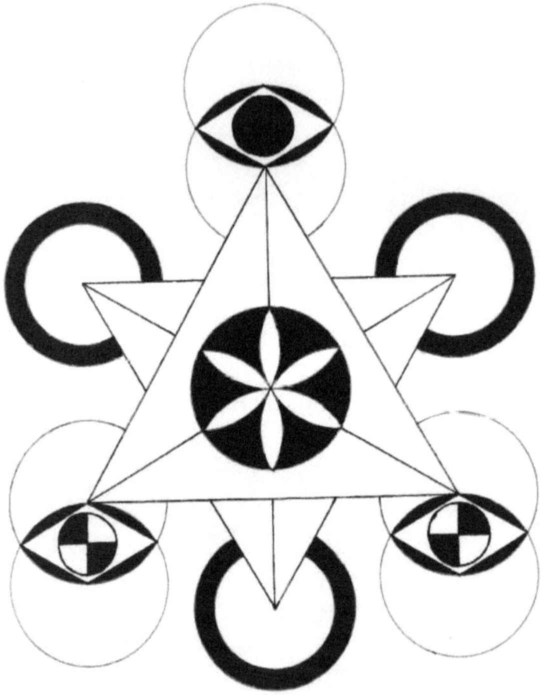

"Vagabond"

Trust in the traveling spirit,
The vision, you can hear it,
Painting pictures, bright and vivid,
If you want love, give it,
This is your life, live it,
I admire your essence,
I'll always admit it,
The truth is…
They'll never get it,
Everyone's a critic,
Who's a creator?
We'll find out sooner than later,
Silence speaks symbols of sanity,
Through the veil of vicious vanity,
Becoming what I planned to be,
Working through insanity,
Can't stand to be sitting still,

Still standing to feel the thrill,

This wisdom is the pill,

Please don't waste your will,

Find your fuel and get your fill,

Moving forward, toward the hill,

From the alleys of the apple valley,

To the mountains of Colorado,

Word around town,

Down by the water,

The nights always get hotter,

Molding the energy like a potter,

Feeling all the love when I spot her,

Daughter of a sorceress,

Daringly dancing in a short dress,

A dashing damsel far from distress,

Mind a mess, don't stress the urgency,

But it's an emergency,

Emerge and see myself in the best of health,

Working with wealth to benefit humanity,

Learning to live, living to learn accordingly.

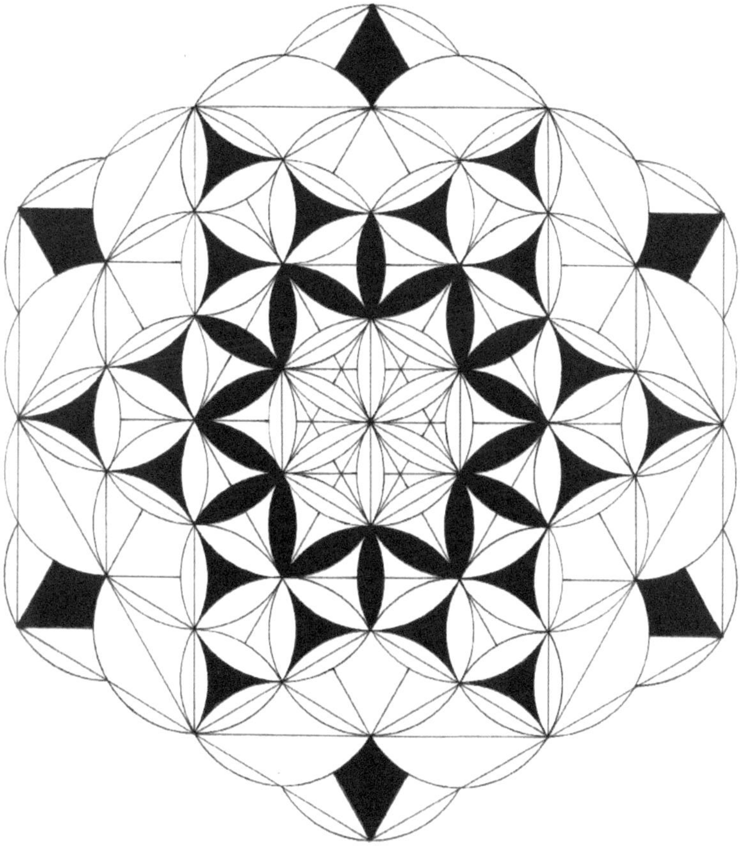

"Dreams"

Nothing is,

As it seems,

These wild dreams,

Papers piled,

Streams of consciousness,

Working on responsiveness,

Feelings of faith,

Facing the intimidation,

Imitating limitation,

Anxious anticipation,

As the energy escalates,

A message emanates in my mental mansion,

Extensive expansion,

Excessive expression,

Death to depression,

As the suppression stops,

Support starts the art of multiplying,

This life is simply satisfying,
Giving to the living is gratifying,
Symbols for sharing gratitude and graces,
As we connect through common places,
Spacious spaces,
Relaxing at the races,
Saints and Sinners,
Conversing over dinners,
Discussing details of dancing diamonds,
Daring demons staring,
Scheming, Dreaming,
Teeming with a lust for light,
Night has just begun,
A heist of dreams,
A mystifying magician makes 3 from 1,
A moment of confusion,
Impulse and Illusion,
Honestly, there was none,
The master of mystery,
The mystery of the master,

Will we ever know?

We reap and we sow,

We're always moving, even if it's slow,

Focused on the movements to grow,

The wind starts to blow,

Moving on, that's all we know,

On the land is shining snow,

In my mind, a silent flow,

In design, I'm letting go,

These passionate pieces appear,

From the fear I let go,

"you're the one chasing your dreams",

She says,

It's not what it seems,

Flowing with the streams,

Following my curiosity,

Mind bursting at the seams,

Eyes shining like headlight beams,

Calling forth teams of leaders,

In love,

Gifted a golden heart,
Art from above,
Below the surface,
I found a purpose,
Patiently watching seeds of passion grow,
Allowing life to flow naturally,
Trusting what I know,
"These blessings are after me"
She sat speechless,
Her eyes spoke to me,
The beginning of a beautiful book,
A look, like "love",
A shook white dove,
She left me curious,
A need to read more,
A foreign feeling,
As she walked out the door,
Heart hit the floor,
Scary, she was far from ordinary,
A few seconds of forever,

I could spend every day learning more,
I'm a kid and she is my candy store.
Swimming in her ocean eyes,
Seeing that her love never dies,
She speaks,
My heart flies,
Mind trying to comprehend,
The beauty of her being,
She's adorable and wild,
Her love is a drug,
She's got to go,
I'm high and feeling low,
Moving slow,
As the wind starts to blow,
I'm adrift, pull me to shore,
Whatever you give,
I promise there's more,
It's your laugh that I adore,
It's even cute when you snore,
That smile is to die for,

In my dreams we walk the sandy shore,
Moments come, moments go,
Familiar faces, some I know,
Similar places, watch them grow,
I've seen this before,
Heard there's more in store,
Still on the floor,
Another night, up till four,
Through the pen,
My heart will pour till the day I soar,
Love seems to leave me sore,
I still crave more,
Riches galore and I still feel poor,
I feel like I'm missing something,
Or someone,
Longing for the long embrace,
Gazing at a lover's face,
A beautiful woman whose steps…
Set fire to the place as she sets the pace.

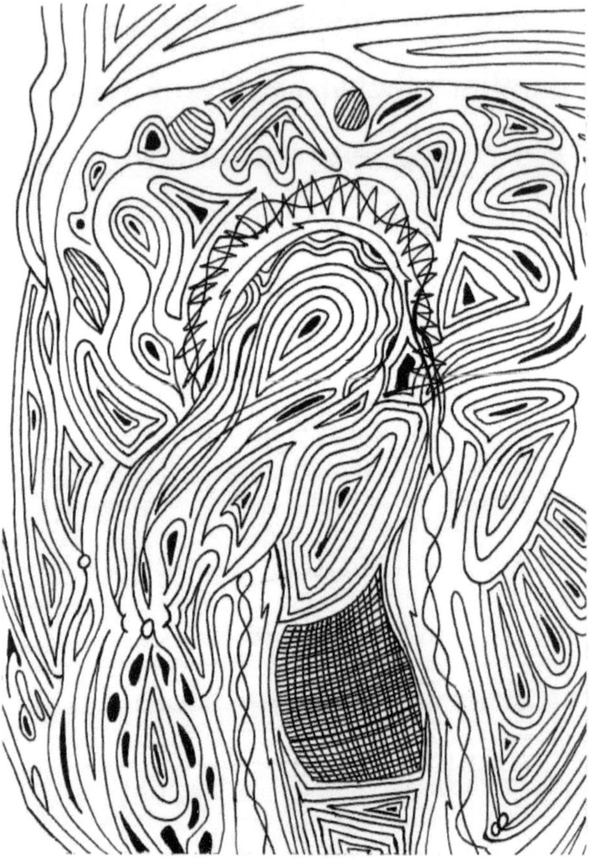

"Deadlines"

We give ourselves deadlines,
Times when it's ok to give up,
Like our lines are dead,
All the "time" is in your head,
Don't listen, don't fret,
Let your smile glisten, without regret,
It's safe to bet, my intentions are set,
This is the healing, I've got a feeling,
Way beyond the ceiling,
Peeling off the mask,
With the questions I ask,
A tempting task,
To taunt the terror,
As if I wasn't looking in a mirror,
The image getting clearer,
I see the light for what it is,
For it is all,

Standing, staring,

Stone-like and spacious,

Grateful and gracious,

These deadlines seem like headlines,

Seconds strangling streams of information,

Inflammation from stressful head vines,

Squeezing at the source,

Excessive force,

A challenging course,

A wild horse,

The stable,

We're here,

Willing and able,

Rewriting the fable before it hits the table,

After a long day, we hit the hay,

Silence and stillness as we pray,

Pay my dues,

I must rest, so I lay to snooze,

Displace my space to cruise,

Turning knew to news,

Burning blues and break throughs,
Putting miles on these old shoes,
Wandering through the streets,
I peruse magazines of melancholy madness,
Everyone serenading their sadness,
Ignoring helping hands of happiness,
A common competition,
Racing repetition,
The definition of insanity,
Slaves to the vanity,
Victimizing their sanity,
A creator's calamity,
Didn't plan to be,
A part of the art taking place,
This empty space,
Occupied by words of grace,
Chaos, among the order of nature,
Nature, among the chaos of order,
A chain of command,
Demanding rain upon the land,

A grain of the finest sand,

A faceted fractal honoring the holy hand,

The smallest pieces are still pieces,

Precisely placed to perform their purpose,

Disregarding the tiny blessings,

Dressing our days,

Stressing the plays,

Wondering which of them pays the most,

Money doesn't make art,

But art makes everything,

The shadows of nothing,

I know they're bluffing,

Stuffing lies in the eyes of lovers,

A healing hand hovers,

The feeling of fire flutters,

The engine of inspiration sputters,

Drowning in ideas,

Patiently waiting on motivation,

He's the king of procrastination,

Never lacks an explanation,

Always lurking at the station,
Distracting deeds of imitation,
Time for initiation,
Address the situation,
"We need cooperation,
Connecting communication,
Communicating connection,
This a reflection,
Changing the direction",
Bright and early,
We fire the machine,
We'll hire a whole team,
An empire from a dream,
A vision in the steam,
A bath in the stream,
A new day brought to life,
My wealth is my wife,
Dancing from day to night,
Creating as energy turns to light.

"Tell apathy"

If we own these thoughts,

They surely own us,

Who's to say, that they are ours,

Everything in question,

Morals and telepathy,

Electricity and empathy,

She saw the best of me,

Talking of a recipe,

Working on the rest of me,

Blessed to be,

In the presence of an angel,

She shines her light in every angle,

Unpredictable and fun,

Heart shining like the sun,

A magnet of miracles,

Attracting, distracting,

Impacting,

The mirror of my mind,
Shattered,
Pieces, Pieces,
Peaceful pieces,
The puzzle remains puzzling,
Guzzling information,
A life of constant stimulation,
Certainly, a simulation,
Dedication to education,
Learning to love,
Loving to learn,
Let the fire burn,
Admire your flames,
As the arrow aims,
Fate proclaims protection,
A narrow passage,
A sparrow passes,
Lungs filled,
Feelings spilled,
Thrilled, but my heart is chilled,

This place...
Mind starts to race,
STOP.
Remember... she's an ace,
Setting pace with a smile on her face,
Grasping on to glances of her grace,
She advances without a trace,
Sketching her silhouette,
Shadows we'll never forget,
We'll meet in mystery,
Don't discuss the history,
The weakness of the walls,
Calls to all who worship old wounds,
Ignoring the new tunes,
Bright balloons,
The party of a lifetime,
The life of time at a party,
Perception of perspectives,
Planning to prosper,
Proposals of peace.

"Ease"

Focus on the craft,
Floating on the raft of life,
Resting through the rapids,
Nesting among captives,
Captions contain criticism,
Staring at these words,
Hearing a rhythm,
Watching a movie,
Perspective is reflective,
A selective objective,
Free the collective,
Focused like a flashlight,
Shining bright in the night,
Sights of fights,
Lights and rites,
Sacred circles,
Holy ground,

Pass the horn around,
Hail the gods before us,
Prospering against the odds,
Blessings forever multiply,
Looking to the sky,
As she starts to cry,
Doubts die,
As we learn to fly,
Wings of gold,
Tales are told,
A family,
Young, but old,
Confident and bold,
Behold, kindred,
An ocean of opportunity,
Open to the whole community,
Promotion of commotion,
Peace turns to unity,
Loving with impunity,
Laughing at the similarity.

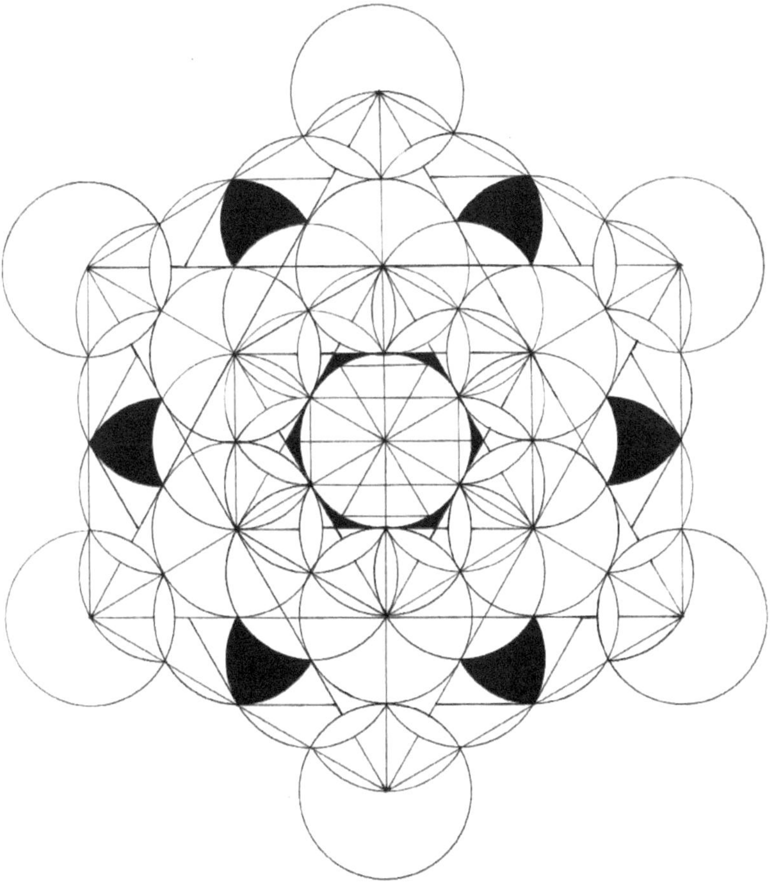

"Abundance"

Things come naturally,

Stings,

Sentimental strings actually,

Preachers, teachers, creatures,

Abundant beings,

Seeing spectacular scenes,

Flying fast through daily dreams,

Slowing down to view the variety,

Simply searching,

A scared society,

Shy of sincerity,

Creatively comparing,

Crafting confidence,

Drafting delicate delivery,

Embracing electricity,

Abundance in the air,

This feeling is rare,

A steady stare,
Everything is multiplying,
Ideas, intentions,
Actions of inspiration,
Currents of creation,
Sensation,
Anticipation,
Frames by the fraction,
Lights, camera,
Action,
Attraction to reaction,
A faction of fearless fellows,
Focused on faith,
Fears of freedom falter,
Placing the self on the altar,
These pieces bring peace,
The conflicts cease,
Waves of prosperity,
Transparency,
Crystal clear clarity,

Everything is "here" and "now",
I hear it now,
I hear it loud,
The abundance of potential,
A differential,
A degree of difference,
Destiny and deliverance,
The wealth of all that is,
Is there,
When the sun is out,
We stare,
Light is information,
Tune in to the station,
The source is the source,
Abundant and glowing,
His radiance showing,
Always keep going,
Never stop growing,
An attitude of gratitude,
Keep the blessings flowing.

"Destiny"

What's meant to be, will be,
We exhaust ourselves mentally,
Physically and spiritually,
Playing fictitious roles,
Paying tolls of "necessity",
A recipe for disaster,
Only a few will master,
"I'm telling you something,
I know nothing",
If we think things through,
We see the ship sink too,
We're planting seeds,
Without pulling weeds,
Will we ever fulfill our needs?
Changing paths,
How do we know where the last one leads?
Moving fast,

Through the past,
Slowing down the moment,
Own it,
The ready one succeeds,
The steady one exceeds,
My pen bleeds for you to read this,
Always remember,
Seek bliss,
After days in the dark,
Your spark will return,
Starting a blaze in your heart,
Changing the ways of your art,
We're here to play a part,
Multiple stages,
A progression through the ages,
The war wages while the fire rages,
Mages and sages come,
Liars run,
As the pages turn,
They burn,

The past goes up in flames,

A story of unforgotten names,

The courageous ones never run,

Faith, shining bright like the sun,

Through the warrior's will the war is won,

The work has just begun,

We won't stop till it's done,

Making love for fun,

Reminiscing days that I had none,

Creating ways through the haze,

A phase we were in,

It pays to sit and spin,

Scratching the surface of success,

There's no gamble,

If the aim is off,

Ramble on,

Till the game is over,

Under the table,

A bet is made,

A debt is paid.

"Resurrection"

Hit the ground running,
Hear the sound, stunning,
Feel the pound, buzzing,
The bees are back,
Eyes are black,
Silly lies of lack,
Prosperity is right on track,
Waters of wealth,
Flowing through every crack,
Blessings begin to stack,
The fact is…
Fearful tactics fill the actors,
Fools following faithless factors,
Fallacies of freedom,
A façade of frailty,
Facing features at festivals,
Creatures of curiosity,

In the darkness,
Shadows dancing,
Rings of fire,
Fierce flames,
People prancing,
One sings to inspire,
A tale of no names,
Seconds of serendipity,
Feelings of fascination,
Gifts of gratitude,
Gentle giants,
Whispers in the wind,
Kindred spirit,
Do you hear it?
Far from death,
Back to life,
Looking forward,
Moving toward the light,
Is it left, or right?
This is flight,

Mind on a mission,
Movies for admission,
Apply your attention,
Ascend the dimension,
Freedom from the tension,
Amplified ascension,
Inspired intention, intervention,
Relief and relaxation,
Energetic elevation,
Creating constantly,
Channeling change,
Currency coursing,
Current sea of energy,
Flowing free,
Activating forces,
Helpful sources,
Healthy horses,
Ready for the races,
Steady stares,
No forgotten faces,

These places emit love,
Shiny spaces of light,
Right in the heart,
Where all things start,
Nothing will replace that part,
Actions of authenticity,
Multiplying mastery,
Magnifying mass to see the detail,
Knowledge will always prevail,
Wisdom of the waters we sail,
The light of love,
Shining above,
Bright and bold,
Peaceful and passionate,
Powerful and passive,
Patient and persistent,
Caring and consistent,
We love,
Your love of light.

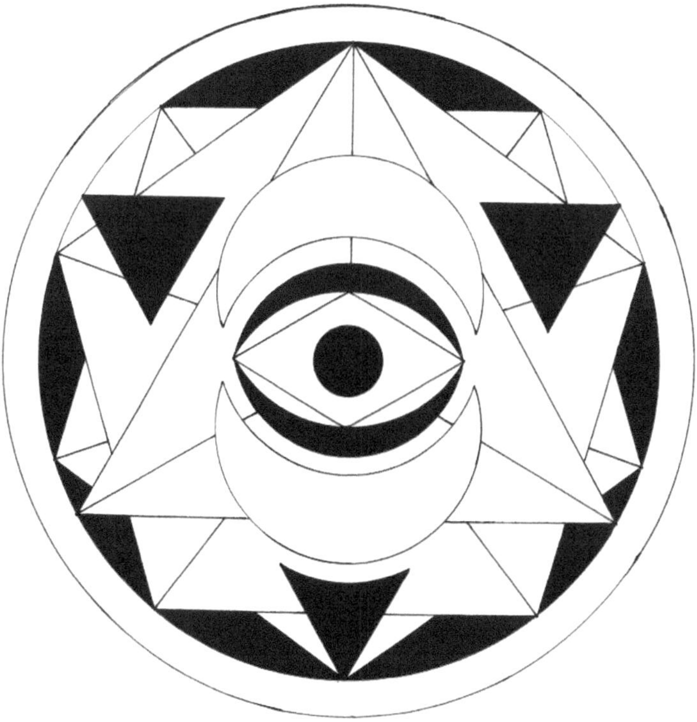

"Choices"

We have a choice,
Raise our voice,
Lower the weapons,
Moving fast,
Past previous deceptions,
Peaceful perceptions,
Powerful praise,
No exceptions,
Magic mirror,
Multiple reflections,
Ideas for inception,
Constant conception,
A channel of change,
A current of currency,
Flowing frequently,
Following frequency,
Symbols in silence,

Volunteers for violence,
Choices, choices,
Value the voices,
Rejoices of revelation,
Clouds of celebration,
Coughing often,
Off in the coffin,
Knocking on the lid,
A connection to the grid,
Deep inside,
A light was hid,
Demons of darkness,
Light would rid,
These words are writ,
Pieces to the puzzle,
They fit,
With the wisdom comes wit,
Motions in the moment,
Quick to hit,
Lick and split,

Flick and sit,

Fire to a fortress,

Enter the forest,

For rest,

No test,

Purely blessed,

A king to a kingdom,

The scents of common cents,

Common sense,

Passion pours prosperity,

Creating clarity,

Confident choices,

Various voices,

A valiant voyage,

The wreckage is a message,

Destruction,

The conduction of change,

Scenes seem strange,

Rearrange,

A new range,

New planes of existence,
Strains of resistance,
Hands of assistance,
Helpful heroes,
An army of angels,
Light from all the angles,
It's showtime,
No time like the present,
Present your presence,
Your essence is holy,
Wholly… Love,
That is,
All that is,
Above and below,
Seeds start to grow,
Staring through the snow,
Trees start to show,
Branches,
Flowers,
Fruit,

Fractal features,
Feed the creatures,
Lead the teachers,
Disperse the details,
Chasing tales of tail is stale,
The free never fail,
Ship is setting sail,
Get a pail, he's getting pale,
Try this ale,
Keep your head off the rail,
Mind on the miracles,
Blind to the blessings at sea,
We see what we look for,
Mistook by the mystery,
A hook in the history,
A book of liberty,
Words of freedom,
Mental bars of management,
Bars bent by bravery,
Overcome the slavery.

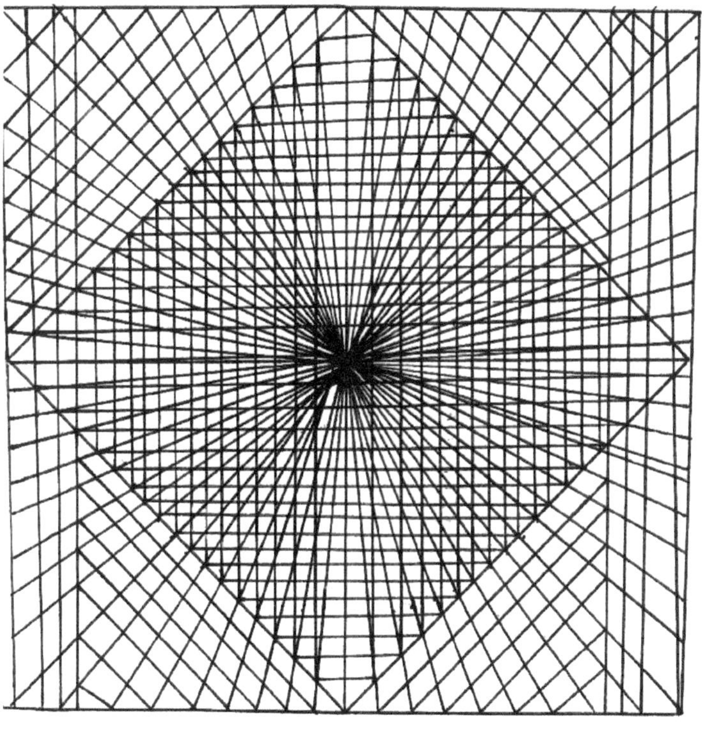

"Liberation"

Free the mind,
Behind the scenes,
A message screams,
Subliminal streams,
These monkeys mess with dreams,
It seems,
The seams are stressed,
Pressed by the best,
Not impressed,
The master's chest,
Invest,
This quest is blessed,
A master's test,
Going through the motions,
Sailing oceans of the self,
Wisdom fills wells with wealth,
Wizards of stealth,

Witches of health,
The magic is miraculous,
Liberation from the body,
Separation of the soul,
Conscious of that which makes us whole,
Mind takes a toll,
Without a rock,
We'd never roll,
A connection to the cosmos,
Mirrors of manifestation,
Looking for a lover,
Never saw the cover,
A few words of the book,
Where to look?
Inside, of course,
Outside the force,
Fear whispers in the ear,
Silently paying attention,
Pure intention,
The façade will falter,

Welcome to the altar,
Praise the passion,
Forgotten fashion,
Steady stashing,
Pieces of peace in passing,
Practice has its purpose,
Patience for the verses,
Preaching for a purchase,
Reaching for the churches,
Leaching from the purses,
Preying on people's property,
Teaching propaganda,
Dividing us properly,
Believe in this, believe in that,
There's no rabbit in the hat,
Contradictions,
Internal conflictions,
Curses cast by creatures,
Leachers of light,
A fear of flight,

This is the night,

A beginning,

Spinning new narratives,

Exploration,

Renovation of the foundation,

Fearless,

Faceted,

Flawless,

Confidence in character,

Effortless ecstasy,

An entity of energy,

Meant to be,

Mentally mysterious,

Spiritually mischievous,

Physically pretentious,

Restless and relentless,

Pressure to prevent stress,

Weaves of worship,

Waves of waiting,

Worth it,

Experiences of eternal expression,

Diving deep,

Depths of depression,

Aggression,

Obsession,

Leading lies to the light,

Riding eyes through the night,

Singing songs of surrender,

A lover and defender,

Through the blender,

An honest heart is tender,

Sporting each scar,

Bearing every bar,

Shooting every star,

Friends with fear,

We're going real far,

Cruising in the car,

Joy in a jar,

Books in a backpack,

Blazing trails, don't back track,

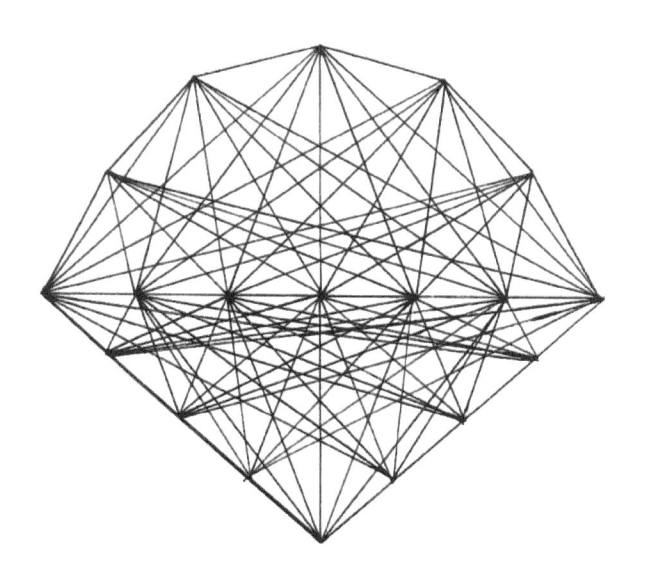

"Creation"

The sensation,

Creation,

Admiration,

Anticipation,

Participation,

Bringing life to art,

Art to life,

A gift of gratitude,

Along the latitude,

This line of time,

Extended by the rhyme,

Speaking spells,

Silent spaces,

Familiar faces,

Clear the stages,

Turn back the pages,

We're starting over,

Under construction,
Declaration of destruction,
Emotional eruption,
Situations slip away,
Letting go of limitation,
Increase the imagination,
Release frustration,
Creative concentration,
Faithfully focused,
A date with destiny,
A princess,
Dressed to be a peasant,
Blessed by the present,
Aware of the stare,
A gaze,
The mental maze,
A phase of mirrors,
Magic messages,
Mind of miracles,
Miracles of mind,

Manifesting mastery,
A masterpiece of memory,
Story of the century,
Sent to be,
A master key,
Close calls of catastrophe,
Walls of worry weaken,
Opportunities leak in,
Windows of pain,
People peek in,
Seeking,
Speaking,
Peaking on their prey,
Villainous vampires,
Crowds around campfires,
The enemy of energy,
An endless emptiness,
Feeding on friendliness,
Fiends for fame,
Following the frame,

Pleasures of the pain,
Limits of the lane,
These lyrics keep me sane,
Heading home,
Hearing heaven's tone,
Heals the heart of stone,
History unknown,
Geometric throne,
Hone the skills,
Daring drills,
Pairing pills,
Staring at stills,
Thrills from kills,
Death by decompression,
A composition of aggression,
Embrace the expression,
Supply the stares with careless comedy,
A casual commodity,
Oddly forgotten,
The laugh of love,

Laughter,

After anxious answers,

Before the chapter of questions,

Suggestions?

Directions?

Open opportunity,

Close the case,

Space for speculation,

On the chase for contribution,

Relentless retribution,

Energetic evolution,

Raging revolution,

A solitary solution,

Dreams of the daring,

Compassionate and caring,

Staring out windows,

Sights shimmer in the sun's light,

Wisdom whispers as the wind blows.

Thanks for reading,

Leave a review online at:

https://lulu.com/spotlight/artbyant

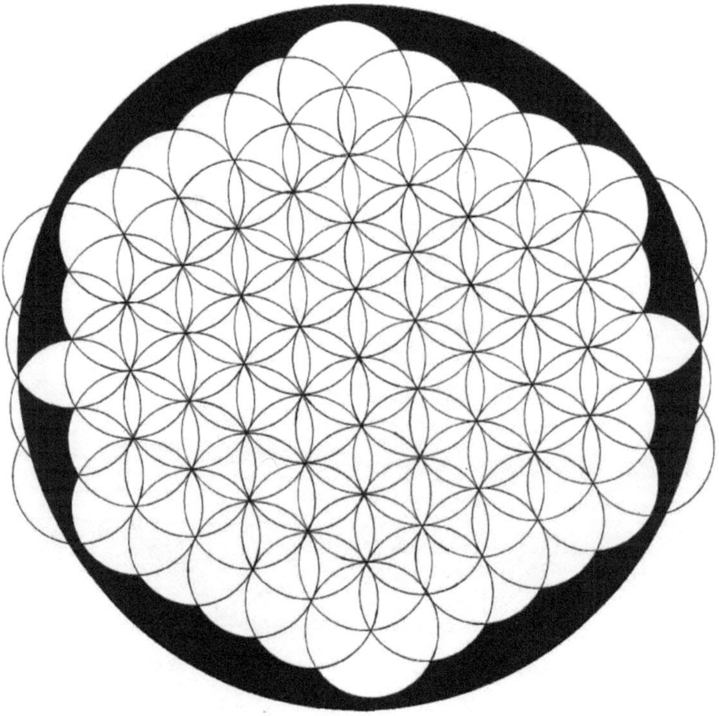